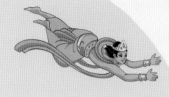

Stories from Faiths
Hinduism

Krishna Steals the Butter
and Other Stories

Library of Congress Control Number: 2007001011

ISBN 978 1 59566 377 1

Written by Anita Ganeri
Design and editorial by East River Partnership
Illustrated by Nilesh Mistry
Series Consultant Roger Butler

Publisher Steve Evans
Creative Director Zeta Davies
Senior Editor Hannah Ray

Printed and bound in China

Stories from Faiths
Hinduism

Krishna Steals the Butter
and Other Stories

Anita Ganeri
Illustrated by Nilesh Mistry

QEB

Rama and the Demon King

Long ago, there lived a prince named Rama. His father was a powerful king. Rama married a beautiful princess named Sita and they were very happy.

4

The king wanted Rama to be the next king. But Rama's stepmother did not like Rama. She sent Rama, Sita, and Rama's brother, Lakshman, to live in a forest, faraway.

One day, a poor, old man came to the cottage
where Rama and Sita lived. Rama and
Lakshman were out hunting. Sita welcomed
the old man and asked him to come inside.

6

But, the old man was really a wicked demon king in disguise. His name was Ravana. Ravana kidnapped Sita and carried her away to his palace.

For many days, Rama and Lakshman looked high and low for Sita. But they could not find her anywhere. They asked the wise monkey god, Hanuman, for help.

Hanuman found Sita in Ravana's palace.
He told Rama and Lakshman, and they
set off to rescue her. They took a great
army of monkeys and bears.

Ravana and his army of giants and demons came to fight Rama and his army. A terrible battle followed. Finally, Rama killed Ravana with a magic bow.

Rama and Sita were delighted to see each other again. They rode back to the royal palace in a huge flying chariot. There they were crowned king and queen.

Krishna Steals the Butter

Once upon a time, there was a little boy named Krishna. He lived in a village in India with his mother, Yashoda, and his father, Nanda.

The village where Krishna lived was very beautiful.
A river flowed through the middle, and the forests
all around were full of peacocks, monkeys, and deer.

One day, Yashoda was making some butter. As she worked, she sang a song that she had made up about Krishna.

Krishna came to find his
mother. Yashoda stopped
work and held out her arms.
She let Krishna sit on her
lap and gave him a big hug.

Suddenly, Yashoda remembered something. She had put a pan of milk on the stove to boil. She left Krishna to check that the milk had not boiled over and spoiled.

Krishna was angry when
his mother left him. He
opened a pot of newly
made butter and ran
off with a big handful!

When Yashoda came back, she discovered that Krishna and the butter were missing. Yashoda followed her son's buttery footprints. She found Krishna in the garden, feeding the butter to the monkeys!

Yashoda told Krishna that he had been very naughty. But, she did not stay angry for very long. She loved Krishna very much, even when he had done something wrong!

Ganesh and the Moon

One day, it was Ganesh's birthday. Ganesh was the elephant god. His mother cooked him a delicious dinner and gave him many of his favorite sweets to eat until his belly was full.

Later that evening, Ganesh went back home, riding on his rat. The moon shone, big and round, in the sky. It was getting quite dark.

Suddenly, the rat stumbled
In the darkness, the rat
had tripped over a snake.
Ganesh fell off with a
thud. But, he was too
full of sweets to
get back on!

Ganesh had an idea.
He caught the snake
and tied it around his
middle, like a belt, to
hold up his tummy.
Then, he carefully
got back on the rat.

Ganesh heard a noise. The moon was laughing at him! Ganesh was so angry that he snapped off his right tusk and threw it at the moon.

The moon went out. With no moon, there was no nighttime and people could not go to sleep. The people begged Ganesh to bring back the moon.

So, Ganesh let the moon shine again. But he did not allow it to be big and round all the time. Sometimes, it was bigger and sometimes it was smaller.

That is why Ganesh the elephant god
only has one tusk. And it is also why
the moon seems to change
shape in the night sky.

The Goddess and the Lotus Flower

Long ago, before the world began, the sea was made of milk. A giant, white lotus flower floated in the middle of the milky sea.

Many precious treasures were hidden in the sea of milk. The gods and demons wanted the treasures, but how could they get them out?

The gods and demons made a plan. First, the gods pulled up a huge mountain. Then, they put the mountain into the sea of milk.

Next, the demons took a gigantic snake. They tied the snake around the mountain. The gods held one end of the snake and the demons held the other.

The gods and demons began to pull the snake
to and fro. As they pulled, the mountain spun faster
and faster. This made the sea froth and foam.

Many wonderful treasures came out of the sea.
Among them was a tree that made wishes come
true and a magical elephant with wings.

Then, a beautiful goddess appeared. Her name was Lakshmi and she was sitting in a lotus flower. Lakshmi held a garland of lotus flowers in her hands.

Lakshmi saw the great god, Lord Vishnu. She took the flower garland and put it around Lord Vishnu's neck. Then, she became Vishnu's wife.

Notes for Parents and Teachers

About Hinduism

Hinduism is perhaps the world's oldest living religion, dating back at least 4,000 years to ancient India. It is a very varied religion with many different ways of practicing, although most Hindus share the same basic beliefs. Instead of "Hinduism," many Hindus prefer to call their religion "sanatana dharma," which means "eternal teaching." They believe that beyond the world we live in (the material world) is Brahman (spirit). Brahman is eternal, unchanging, and everywhere, while the material world does not last and is always changing. Some Hindus called Brahman "God." Hindus believe in one God, but God's different powers, qualities, and forms are represented as many gods and goddesses.

About the stories in this book

In each of the world's religions, stories play an essential part. For centuries, they have been used to teach people about the traditions and beliefs of their religion in an accessible way, making difficult ideas and concepts easier to understand. For children in today's multicultural society, these stories also provide an ideal introduction to the different religious faiths, their key figures, and beliefs.

Rama and the Demon King

The story "Rama and the Demon King" is told in the Ramayana, one of the most important and popular of Hindu works. It is an epic poem with 24,000 verses. The story is particularly remembered in October or November, when Hindus celebrate the festival of Diwali. People decorate their homes and mandirs (temples) with small, clay lamps to guide Rama and Sita home. Rama is an avatar (earthly incarnation) of the god Vishnu, and is one of the most popular Hindu gods, revered for his goodness and courage. His victory over Ravana is seen as the triumph of good over evil.

Krishna Steals the Butter

For many Hindus, Krishna, like Rama, is an avatar of Vishnu and one of the best-loved Hindu deities. For some Krishna devotees, he is the supreme God. Many stories are told about his childhood in the village of Vrindavana in northern India, where he was brought up by a cowherd and his wife. Krishna is usually shown with blue skin, playing a flute. The story of Krishna stealing the butter shows Krishna's mischievous nature.

Despite this, his parents always love and forgive him. Followers of Krishna believe that through devotion to Krishna, a person can escape the problems of this life. His birthday is celebrated in August or September with the festival of Janmashtami.

Ganesh and the Moon

This is one of several stories explaining why Ganesh, the elephant-headed god, has only one tusk. In another story, he broke it off and used it as a pen to write the great Hindu epic poem, the Mahabharata. Ganesh is a very special god for Hindus. He is believed to remove obstacles and is worshiped at the start of any new venture, such as undertaking a journey or moving into a new house. Ganesh's birthday is celebrated in August or September with the festival of Ganesh Chaturthi. In some parts of India, huge images of Ganesh are paraded through the streets, then thrown into the river or the sea.

The Goddess and the Lotus Flower

Lakshmi is the Hindu goddess of wealth, wisdom, and good fortune. The story "The Goddess and the Lotus Flower" tells how Lakshmi was one of a number of divine gifts that appeared from the ocean of milk, which existed before the world began. She appears as the gods and demons are churning an ocean of milk, which was traditionally churned to make butter or cheese and extract an elixir of immortality. Lakshmi is often shown rising from a lotus flower or holding lotus flowers in her hands. The lotus flower is an important symbol in Hinduism, signifying purity and spiritual power.

Further things to do

• Read the stories aloud to the children and ask them questions about what they think the stories mean. Find other stories about Rama and Krishna to read.
• Relate the stories to experiences in the children's own lives. For example, have they ever helped a friend in need, as Hanuman helped Rama? Have they ever felt angry when someone laughed at them, as Ganesh did when the moon laughed at him?
• Decorate the classroom or home for Diwali. The children could make diva lamps from modeling clay and illustrate Diwali cards with scenes from the story. Buy or make some Indian sweets to eat. These are given as gifts at festivals. Investigate other Hindu festivals, such as the birthdays of Krishna (Janmashtami) and Ganesh (Ganesh Chaturthi).